The Essence of My Existence

Also by True Vine Publishing Company

Charge the Walls
His Beauty for My Ashes
I Hear God in My Head
Holy Ghost Explosion
Words of My Mouth, Meditations of My Heart
Season Come
Dare I Ask, What Am I Afraid Of?
Seeds of Greatness
Deliverance
Journeys in the Spirit
Positive Thinking Changed My Life
The 24 Minute Ministry Family Devotional
He Who Finds a Wife
Overcoming the Spirit of Fear
Who are the Many?
Life, My Teacher
On Butterfly Wings
The Other Woman
From the Heart
Positive Response Ensures Spiritual Success
Living Beyond Expectancy
My True Soul
The Oasis Collection
The Rhythm of Cognition
When Boaz Comes
Slow Running Honey
I Don't Look Like What I've Been Through
The Time is Now to Hear My Voice
Desiring to Touch the Unclean
Jesus Child: Urban Poetry: Vol. 1
Dreaming With Audacity

The
Essence
of my
Existence

annehenningbyfield

True Vine Publishing
Nashville, TN

The Essence of My Existence
Anne Henning Byfield
Copyright © 2007 by Anne Henning Byfield

ISBN-10: 0982669402
ISBN-13: 978-0-9826694-0-2

Published by True Vine Publishing Company
P.O. Box 22448
Nashville, TN 37202
www.TrueVinePublishing.org

Printed in the United States of America—First printing

To place orders for more books or get current information on the author, contact us at www.TrueVinePublishing.org and www.annehenningbyfield.org

TABLE OF CONTENTS

INTRODUCTION

POET

I didn't know I
was a poet
when I was little
although I was going
to bed reading
books of poetry
and making my
parents proud
reciting
Dunbar's
when Malinda Sings:
Liza, Liza, bless the Lord.

No one told me
I was a poet
even my mean
English teacher
who almost
put me out of class
because she said
my lines didn't rhyme
and were not neat.
I told her who said
blue had to rhyme
with you
and violets weren't blue
they were purple.

I grew up wishing
I was a poet when I read
Poe, Frost, and Longfellow,
wondering why we only read
Wright, Cullen, and Hughes,
in February.....
strong men keep coming.

One day I almost lost my mind
when Bro. Arna Bontemps
came to class.
I was the only one
who knew who he was.
He almost lost his mind
when I was quoting The Day-Breakers
while he was reading.

He told my mean
English teacher
to keep an eye on me
I was probably a poet.
She said my lines didn't rhyme.
He looked at her
like she was crazy not mean.

I almost thought
I could be a poet
when I heard the sisters read.
Carolyn, Nikki, Ms Brooks
seducing me to read
their poems over and over
like I read the Bible.
Sis Carolyn messed me up
saying MF out aloud
without shame as much
as the Last Poets.
I didn't know poets could
say those words.
My momma didn't either
when she proceeded to
beat me for saying them
and was unconvinced
when I kept saying
I ain't saying it
I am quoting Comrade Carolyn.

Reading Sis. Mari Evans
I knew if God could grant
me one opportunity
let it be a poet
one day
somehow
humming and writing
in the night..

Now I realize poets
don't need any permission
to create;
have unrhymed lines;
they just do
they just are...
....poets.

You are about to read (I hope) a poetry book that I have written. How exciting it is to write these words. It is a journey that has taken a long winding route to get to this conclusion. From earliest memories, I wrote on paper, napkins, back of bulletins, and inside book covers. My mother called them my "little poems." Only God knows where most of them are now because they were not significant to me at the time and good stewardship was not exhibited. Reading and writing became my sustenance. I always had a book, and was always writing my thoughts, although I did not realize they were my thoughts. They were just words to me.

I grew up in a family and community that demanded academic excellence and literary knowledge. We were introduced to great writers and were to be able to recite more than Easter poems but the writings of Henry Wadsworth Longfellow, Edgar Allan Poe, Paul Laurence Dunbar as well as the essays of European scholars. Some had great delight in these competitions, others found them a chore. This was the day of new dresses and ribbons in the hair and the "youngins" showing off their skill. The only bad thing for me was that I often won but my parents would not let me take the prize because I was the pastor's child, and they did not think it was appropriate.

Frequently we would recite (not read) poems we had written. My poems did not pass their litmus test and a continuing struggle remained for several years. The question of who is the first audience for whom you are writing, yourself or others stayed unresolved. Then and for years, I thought my work was not up to others' standard and the poem was not four or eight neat lines with rhyming words. Early I wrote for others and not for me and was unfulfilled like the following one.

> *Children gathering in the park*
> *to run on a whim and a lark*
> *so other children would be found*
> *to play and make happy sounds.*

Slowly a private defiance emerged and over the years my writing cared not for what was considered traditional. It was my poem, my rhythm, my rhyme and not for sharing.

There is a place in Chicago called the Point. All of Chicago's finest and not so finest poets gathered there talking about life issues but mainly the revolution. It was there I would listen for hours to every possible subject. I was introduced directly and indirectly to some of the greatest poets ever. Some became nationally known others only in the area. For the first time my poetry fit because there was no model to fit. These poets were free to express themselves without any intervention, correction or criticism. I would get off from work and rush to hear the newest sound, attack on the government or expression of love. The profundity of their self-expression and non-traditional approach was unknown to me other than the books I read as a child.

It released creative energy and helped with my private thoughts but the nagging notion remained that my rhymes were not good enough. Over years at various settings I would share my private thoughts but the notion that "it" was not good enough was louder than my public sharing and eventually shut down most public performances; other than occasionally reading at coffee houses or sliding them into sermons. This persisted for years. When I would preach or speak I began with a poem of mine, I knew when a poem came it brought personal joy more than the extended spoken word. Often people listening did not know that it was for me such a weighty moment.

I was assigned to pastor a church in Detroit in 1999 and that transition proved rewarding and prolific for poetry and music. The desire for a book of poetry rebirthed. This dream could not become reality without being concerned about what others think. It still took me another four years to be committed to the discipline of completion, "oh what a concept".

Now you are about to read (I hope) my book. It is literally the essence of my existence and the meanderings of a journeying spirit. Asante Sana to the Triune God for the gift of being driven to write. Living to write is finally the truth revealed in me as life itself. It's my poem that I want to share. As you read you will notice names at the bottom of the page, they serve as the inspiration of that particular poem.

I appreciate my family and friends who have nurtured this ongoing poem by tolerating my lateness because I had to write, writing when I was to be engaged in conversation and then writing became the conversation. I am grateful even when I complained about being asked to write something at the last moment for an event they participated in. It was a challenge I enjoyed although at times I felt overworked. The list is long but must be acknowledged: my parents, Herman William and Elizabeth Miller Henning, my sisters and brothers: Zettie, Herman, Garnett,

Yvonne, John Patrick, and George; special sisters, Mita, Ernestine, Rita, and Cynthia; Marguerite Butler, Georgina Leavell, Florance McElroy, Pat Efiom; and Nichele Washington, Tameka Surrett and Marcus Scott who God sent to help with the practicality of this project. To Dr. Mari Evans who God sent as wisdom's voice and whose poetry still brings chills to me. Her voice will never be muted in me or in others.

Of course to Ainsley my husband who has endured early morning writing and the destruction of so many trees; Michael my son whose writing skills are yet to be tapped and Miles my grandson all life's witness, love and support give good opportunity for poetry.

Now....

Let your poem
rise up
inciting
with
insight
and
integrity.

I AM POEM

Is Your Cell Phone On?

We have been inundated with intimate stories about Mayors, and Governors gathered from text messages, cell phone records, e-mails, and credit card bills. Big brother is not only watching but uses that information for their advantage. One can argue that those who break the law must be held accountable. At some level that is true.

How many spouses have been caught cheating because their cell phone was left on, or business deals gone awry when unsuitable conversations were overheard. Recently a less than bright kid bragged on his phone that he had cheated on his test. The problem was that the young man had called his father instead of a friend.

Often our own words cause us difficulty either by our foolishness or by the foolishness of others. The Patriots' Act used to identify terrorists has in some cases made terrorists out of persons by the misuse of their words. Sermons, speeches or casual conversations have been listened to and in some instances taken out of context with a "gotcha" mentality.

We cannot let others intimidate us to speak the truth to power. Information technology works both ways. We cannot live in fear about the truth we speak when the Holy Spirit directs us. We must always be reminded that our spiritual enemy will do whatever to discredit our words and actions. We must speak truth to power.

James 1:19 says everyone must be swift to hear, slow to speak, and slow to wrath. We must adhere to that word not out of intimidation but with understanding that someone is always trying to entrap. Let's not help them with thoughtless foolish words whether on the cell phone or any medium. God's button is always on and is listening, and we must be careful what we do or say. Even in our mistakes, God is ever present and walks with us. Your cell phone is always on. Handle it wisely.

This Is My Poem (for Helaine)

This is my poem:
my words,
my rhyme,
my thoughts,
& my perspective.
You do not have
to agree,
accept,
affirm,
approve, or
understand;
just realize that
this is my poem
emanating out of my experience,
radiating from my energy,
originating at my birth,
flowing from my essence
into my existence.
It does not
have to be sublime,
awe-inspiring,
engaging,
or match
your rhythm/style.
It's my poem:
the ode of my imagination;
the sonnet of my thoughts;
the cadence of my lilt,
and at times
the elegy of my decisions.
Still it is
my poem.
enjoy,
relax,
chill,
cry,
laugh.
Don't over process.
Let it induce you to write
your own poem.

I LIKE ME

Now hear ye. Hear ye. Hear ye.
I have an announcement.
No it is a pronouncement.
I have decided,
reached the conclusion,
not made in seclusion,
or out of derision,
or in delusion
I like me...all of me.
I just like me.

It's been a long time coming
around the bend,
when I thought
my self hating days
would never end.
Right now... I like me.
The twisted hair,
fried and slapped
to the side,
weaved,
braided,
wig wearing,
locked,
bold and sassy me.
African centered rapping,
womanist believing,
charismatic worshipping,
hip hop liking,
poetry writing,
Target shopping,
Misook wearing,
saved, filled with the Holy Ghost
preaching, teaching,
imperfect, perfecting me.
Free and seventy three,
fine and twenty nine,
fabulously fashionable fourty,
witty, charming fifty

I just like me.
This is not made
in arrogance
or casual passivity,
not even in personal mediocrity,
ambiguity
or self esteem philosophy.
Just a discovery
and my prerogative
that there is a God
outside of me
who lives in me,
created me,
and on the day
of my conception
before my entrance
into humanity
said, " I like me".

Ain't gonna let nobody
stop me from liking me.
no 90 pound blonde waif.
      250 pound buff brother.
      self hating sister.
No philosophy.
image.
past failures
or broken relationships.
Ain't gonna let my burdens
down by the riverside
inhibit me,
stall me,
frustrate me,
stop me,
destroy me,
make me hate me.
Nothing can get in the way.
My imperfection
will not become
more dominant
than my perfection,
for I like me.

With God I am
a whole number.
Let no man
or woman disagree.
Come here all of you
and recognize one
of the greatest
wonders of the world-me.

Isn't it about time
for you and God
to rhyme;
for you to
take back your mind
and like you
like God likes you and
I like me!
Now hear ye. Hear ye. Hear ye.
I have an announcement,
no it is a pronouncement.
I have decided,
reached the conclusion
not made in seclusion
or out of derision
or in delusion
I like me

I WANT IT ALL

I want it all.
I make no apology that
living below God's means
is not my choice.

Life is about choices
and I choose to have it all,
power, passion
prosperity, peace,
marriage and fulfillment
(why be married and be unhappy
when I can be single and satisfied?

I offer no pretense
or suggest some
inappropriateness
of my desire
to live large.

I'm grown enough,
endured enough,
and lived through
bad choices enough
that my quest is to
have what I want,
when I want it,
how I want it,
and live life to the
fullest God will
give and allow.

You cannot define
my limitations and horizons.
Your opinion
about my choices
may be received
but seldom solicited.
Your concern
whether this is selfish,
self serving,

and greedy
will be noted but
not deter my determination
to have it all.

Chateaubriand, cordon bleu, and
a plate of chitterlings
every now and then,
while listening to
Ne-Yo and dem.
I want BB king,
Beethoven,
Be Be Winans,
Kanye,
Kirk Franklin,
and Corinne Bailey Rae.
Platinum over
fabulous fakes
sitting at the
kitchen island
sipping lemonade/mojitos
on my island
while running
my company
with enough stockings
that I can
use finger nail polish
for my nails not my hose
and know if I go
on a spending spree
I still can pay bills and
have money in the bank.
I want it all.

To bless and be blessed,
give and be given to,
love and be loved,
health and wealth,
spiritual piety, and political power,
intellect, and inspiration,
because I believe
If I decree a thing

it will be established.
Ask anything in my name
and it shall be given to you.

I do not want to die
and have to face God
about the missed opportunities
for greater blessings;
knowing that there
are people assigned
to help me get it all
and I lived below my means
because I did not
actively, aggressively
work the plan.

Achsah: Judges 1/Joshua

RIGHT NOW

This is a grown up epiphany.
I have finally realized that if
I do not become the life I want,
right now,
I will never become.

Right now, today
is my new beginning.
It is up to me
to make the decisions I need to make.
It's time to
forget about past mistakes and successes
and not be trapped by
fear,
other's approval,
time, or
over processing.

Today,
right now
I will live.

Ecclesiastes 11

ONE OF A KIND

Astonishingly amazing,
Courageously creative,
Incredibly ingenious,
Daringly different,
Marvelously mindboggling,
Boldly, one of a kind!

REAL POWER

Real power
comes when we
finally realize
that we have
divinity in our dust
made in the image of
an awesome, beautiful,
powerful God,
who speaks a word
forms the world,
creates
refines,
heals,
resurrects,
takes nothing
and makes
something good
who can do
anything but fail.

When we are
in the image of God,
we are Black,
beautiful,
and strong.

Genesis 1: 26-28

POSITION FOR GREATNESS

*Some of us
have come
to church
for so long
that we have
missed the
awe of
        an awesome God,
the giving
        of a generous God,
the magnificence
        of the Majestic One
and the power
        of an Omnipotent force.
Somehow
        the monotony
        of a routine
        church service,
        powerlessness
        of our prayer lives,
        the repetitiveness
        of church calendars,
        the fashion show,
        annual tea,
        usher program,
        hattitude,
        youth car wash,
        annual barbeque
        our own lack of money,
        healing, peace,
        and power
        we forget that
        there is
prosperity in scarcity,
possibilities in our visions,
realities in our prayer requests,
and even in exile
God is not through blessing God's people
and will position us for greatness.*

Genesis(Issac)

JENDAYII

There are times in which
God answers prayers
with such largesse
that it defies our own
conception and comprehension.
We are given the opportunity
to drink the sweet nectar blend
of vision and reality.
Yet we still have to
crush the grapes, and
make the wine.

Enjoy the work.
I am.

DEFINITION: ALL BECAUSE OF EVE

If you could define yourself,
what would you call yourself:
smart, cute, pretty, soft,
good dresser, daughter, girlfriend,
mother, wife, sister, friend, or nice.
How about mean, nasty, evil,
got an attitude,
can't get along with no one.
Would it be a word
of your own descriptions
or someone else's?
Whose words are you
repeating in your description?

After listening to the
same help tapes
TD Jakes'
"woman thou are loosed 20 times",
not withstanding
all the women's retreats,
women conferences,
or the fact that
you have not missed
a women's day for 10 years.

You still cannot
define yourself,
know...
love...
yourself
walk in peace,
You have heard
that God loves
you unconditionally
and you are
fearfully and wonderfully made.
But it is still hard
for you to say
God loves me

without but words
still resounding.
But
　　　　I am fat.
God has the best for me,
　　　　but I never finished college.
God forgives me,
　　　　but I still had this
　　　　baby without a husband.
God wants to use me,
　　　　but I can't take a man's place.

BUT
I am too bold,
too sassy,
too independent.

What do you say
about you?
Whose report
do you believe?
Have you gotten
to know you?
Have you heard
the voice in you?
Or are you listening
to someone else?

Genesis 3

DARE TO BELIEVE

Dare to believe
that you can have more
than you ask or think.
You are a child of the Most High God,
and nothing is impossible for you.
conceive it,
believe it,
speak it,
initiate action
so that you can achieve it.
Embrace the fullness of God's power
and presence in you
know that God is ready to act
make real
what God has planned for you
in all parts of your life.
This is the day of new beginnings.
Live and bring forth life.

Ephesians 3:20

◆ ◆ ◆ ◆ ◆ ◆ ◆ ◆ ◆ ◆

DOGS FIGHTING

I
saw
two
dogs
fighting.
I
thought
of
you.

Who
are
you
tearing
up
now?

WAKING UP

Waking up
again with
the
intoxicating
invigorating
overpowering
empowering
confrontational
engaging
unforgiving
loving
stimulating
addictive
poem

JUST BECAUSE
I
lost weight
don't mean
I
just got
cute.

Cute
is an
internal thing
and
weight don't
change
what you
feel inside.

AN EVENING WITH ME

An evening with me...
is a wonderful
opportunity.
Con- ver-sat- ting,
re- lax-at-ting,
med-i-tat- ing,
sip-ping
a cup of tea,
reclaiming
harmony,
renewing
energy,
regaining
liberty,
joyous
ecstasy
in community
with me.

I AM BLACK

LORD, WHY DID YOU MAKE ME BLACK?

Several years ago, a six year old girl asked me if God answered prayer. I gave her the preacher's response, of course. She then asked me if I would pray that God would make her white. It took me a moment to regroup and explain that God would not answer that prayer. Her eyes showed that even at her early age, she had pain in her blackness.

Self hatred is not always considered a sin but a sociological or psychological problem. This is a partial truth. Actually, it is a spiritual issue. The word salvation (soteria) means wholeness, well being, soundness, harmony or oneness with God. When we say that you are saved, we are actually saying that you are one with God through the Lord Jesus Christ. The major benefit of that oneness is life abundant and life eternal.

Psalm 100 says in part, it is God who made us and not we ourselves. Genesis 1 says we are made in God's image. Psalm 139 says we are fearfully and wonderfully made. Yet many people particularly African Americans suffer with the truth and reality of that concept because of the impact of racism.

When a six year old girl has already declared that it is better to be white, it means that the images of television, other media outlets, and the treatment in general has had a profound impact. This is even more tragic when African American parents try to live a healthy positive life before them.

We must affirm the mandate God gives to Isaiah in chapter 45:12, "I made the earth and created humankind upon it; it was my hands that stretched out the heavens and I commanded all their host." God loved us so much that he intently made us Black, woman, man, short, tall, married or single. It becomes our spiritual mandate to walk in harmony with God's creative vision for us. Let us work that the sin of self hatred will be killed in us and through us. We are black and proud aloud.

WHEN IS IT OK TO DISOBEY

When it is ok to disobey?
When do we break
Rewrite
Ignore
the rule.
In the cause of liberation
do we say at any cost,
by any means necessary?

When is it ok to disobey?
Does it have to be
a big rule/ big policy?
can we break
a little one
ignore a practice
that creates hardship
and havoc?

Is there a time
in the cause of human justice
that all boundaries are off?

When do we do
what we need to do
in the cause of freedom
and equality!
When is it ok to disobey?

Do we understand
why a 17 year old Palestinian
puts a bomb around her body to go
kill a 17-year-old Israeli
who looks just like her
but lives very differently?
When and if is it ok for a
10-year old gun toter in Liberia,
12-year old knife carrier in
Honduras,
14-year old drug runner in Korea,
15-year old gang member

in south central Detroit?
What do we do about the children
killed in every city USA
who have only known
While living through poverty,
neglect,
harassment,
neighborhood imprisonment
because of color,
gender,
or economic status?

When do we say no?
to white capitalist millionaires
 prostituting the talents
of black boys with gold teeth
low pants and good rhymes
giving them enough to make them
feel empowered while they take
the real gold
to their banks.

When do we ever refuse
to buy the record
because it is sick,
oppressive and destructive
go on the stage
and pull our sisters
and brothers off
and tell them - NO.
Stop shaking your
three-quartered naked behind
and find another way to make it.

When do we tell them
that a new rule that
makes us submissive
to someone else's dominance
is just as bad
as the old one
even if we get just a little
more money than before.

Esther 1: Vashti

WHO'S THE CRIMINAL?

Socrates stole from Imhotep.
European Scholars raped Timbuktu.
White politicians keep raping black women.
Black Men are still lynched physically and by
every area of society.
Elvis Presley takes his music from Little Richard and dem
Justin Timberlake takes it from anybody Black and gets the music award.
The president of Harvard disses Cornel West... can you believe he dissed Cornel
West?
They, not us, took the tanzanite from Tanzania,
the gold from Ghana,
the diamonds from South Africa,
the people from Africa, tortured, made them slaves and killed at random,
oil from the Middle east and Africa,
fine silk and gems from Asia,
and the land from Native Americans,
and yet we are called
ignorant,
heathens,
and criminals.
Go figure.

TUPAC

TuPAC is in the room.
Or at least his revolutionary intelligent
rhyming spirit is in the room.
Without being a thug, drug dealer or
sexually indiscriminate
there must be a new Tupac in the room.
Cause that brother is dead and with
Elvis has left the building.
How those bullets were speedin
that brother ain't breathin,
but his spirit is still in the room.
We need someone to sell
a ghetto gospel
with Christ as center
not violence.
Some one who understands violence
without being violent.
Who refuses to be silent
and will defy,
confront,
denounce,
the violence that begets violence
and the hypocrisy
that brings misery.
Not ashamed of being strange
for truth, and honesty
and real community.
Where is the new Tupac cause
Tupac is dead y'all and
like Elvis has left the building.
How those bullets were speedin
that brother ain't breathin.
But someone is here who can rap
without
calling me a ho,
grabbing my breast,
holding their crotch
can Speak the Truth without fear
respond to violence without guns

know power without being a thug
and can end their rhyme with
Christ lives
Christ died
Christ lives again
Christ will save
Is Tupac's spirit is in the room?

YOU ARE OUR SONS

You are our sons.
Regal, resplendent and spirit tall
displaying the nobility of your ancestors
by bespeaking the passion of greatness
while through the pain of being a
Black man in America.

You are our sons.
Intrinsically brilliant, incredibly intelligent,
naturally pure and powerful,
fusing strength, sensitivity, and sensuality
with such prowess that others can only
gasp with respect when you enter the room.
Take your place in life and history.
Walk in your manhood.
Rejoice, you have divinity in your dust.
Exude the essence of your creation.
Persuasive, prosperous and purposeful.

Breathe out the potency of your re-creation
that you are free despite society's boundaries
and can do/be whatever God and you say
for whom the Lord sets free is free indeed.
Survive, thrive and live.
You are our sons.

YOU ARE OUR DAUGHTERS

You are our daughters.
Resolute and respected,
living out the legacy
of the ancestors before you.
You are our daughters.
Bold and beautiful,
bragging of the creator's imagination
every time you enter the room.
You are our daughters.
Tall and talented,
gifted and graceful,
declaring
you shall live
when the truth is spoken to you.
Rise my daughters rise
in the image of your womanness.
Stand my daughters stand
in the strength of your mothers and sisters.
Shake off the lies and loathings of your essence.
Shout the glory of your
purpose,
potential
and liberation.
You are our daughters.

IT' S YOUR TIME

The heavens have commanded,
the earth has responded,
to the call for men to
lift up holy hands,
celebrate the goodness of God,
declare their loyalty to Jesus Christ and
set their faces like flint
proclaiming that they are not afraid of the ungod
and will use their blood bought authority to:
take back families, church and community;
increase the brotherhood of believers;
give witness that;
saved holy ghost filled brothers are
visionaries,
creative,
prophetic,
worshippers
loving
an astounding,
amazing,
incredible
God.

MY MAD HAT

I must admit that right now
I am like Job with some anger issues.
My own version of
the Mad Black Woman's Syndrome.
Not because my man's gone ,
can't get a date,
my hair did not turn out right,
or I hate my momma.
Tired of
ill prepared, ill read,
no thinking persons who
want to make me deny that
I am Black, Woman, and Methodist.
ill prepared, ill read,
one-dimensional religionists
who pronounce AME A ME E
Episcopal- Epispapal
and now are experts
on the episcopacy.
King James Version/ Matthew Henry
reading only who cannot pronounce
the words they quote
getting their theology
from television preachers
with their great revelation
that the reason
there is so much homosexuality
in the black community
because black women
do not love their men like Delilah did....
Just when you think that
you had it all worked out
and excited to be the son or daughter
of the Lord Jesus Christ
here comes the head of the Holy Ghost Temple Church, of the First Born Deliv-
ered, Church of Christ, Apostolic Tradition with Methodist/Baptist leanings who
do not have African American women in their pulpit now waving in front of us
white women preachers who tell me how to be free.
It is bad enough that we have to

contend outside the body of Christ,
but now we have to contend inside the church.
Sisters who invite us for their women's day,
make us feel respected, and accepted.
Dem same sisters will vote
against or reject a woman as pastor.
Making theological
what is really sociological and anthropological.
Mad I tell you...
ill prepared, ill reading,
no thinking persons
who know Black history from the internet.
Lerone Bennett wanna bees.
Carter G. Woodson ain'ts.
Those ain't walked in our parents shoes.
Ain't raised 10 children and none went to jail.
Don't know what it means to take one chicken
and feed a multitude.
did not quit a job
because the white man made them mad.
These new philosophers
teach new principles
that sound just like the old stuff.
Sounds of Job's friends.
The problem with Black folks is Black folks-
not the impact of historical racism.
Sexism is not a problem,
women must learn to stay in their place.
People are poor because they choose to be
and that everything bad that happens to us comes out of our fault.

Suffering,
pain,
neglect,
poverty,
poor education,
Somalia
tsunami ,
Sudan,
AIDS
all our fault
their only other response

---

is some stupid clichés.
This is only a test for your testimony;
You are not stressed but blessed;
You are blessed and highly favored;
When you tell them I am blessed
but I am still stressed
and blessed and highly favored
meant that Mary was pregnant
outside of wedlock
and was about to be killed,
they just stare at you, cause it's your fault.
I'm mad like Job
but then I decided
to read the end of the book.
Now I have a word for ill read, ill-prepared people.
I have hope in the worst of circumstances,
the greatest of suffering, and assault.
It is God that still will have the last word.
This is not the end of the story.

IS IT JUST ME?

Is it me
or has the world
gone stark raving mad?
Is there anyone
who thinks it's odd
for young men
and women on the stage
with no clothes on
holding their crotches
acting out the
most perverted of sex acts
and then when they finish saying
I just want to
give God the thanks
and my Lord and
Savior Jesus Christ
he's my main homey?
Is it just me?

Don't you think
that it is a little strange
for Puffy Combs, P Diddy, Puff Daddy
to make a song about the wildest
kind of sex and then
go on the religious station singing
about
how he and God are tight.
Jesus gave him the love
while he is parading
his girlfriend
with no clothes on?

Or Lil Kim who brags that
she has had no sex in several weeks
saying Praise God after
she has acted out the
vilest of sex acts on television.
Is it just me?

How about conservatives who say we
need to
do something about all these abor-
tions
cause we are killing the babies
yet will not vote to raise a penny
for education,
employment training
or health benefits.
Then there are those
would be historians,
neighborhood intellectuals
who know all about
what is right for the country.
Which politician should be elected
yet will not vote,
go to a town meeting
or help on election day.
Is it just me?

Can you hear them talking about
'dem poor starving people in Africa"
"dem tsunami victims in Asia"
And "dem bad kids in America
and will not discipline
their own children,
go to a PTA meeting
or give to or work for a mission cause
to help" dem people"
Is it just me?

PRISON VISIT 1

number
I'm sorry
number
Number-inmate number
Id
excuse me
(long sigh)
your state issued driver's license
here it is
sign in
yes.
you can't wear jewelry
not at all
wedding ring
just my wedding ring
yep
I need to go back to the car and put
it.....
locker
excuse me
put it in the locker
where?
there
quarter.
excuse me?
IT COST A QUARTER!
I'm sorry this is my first time.
I still need to go back to the car and
get money
You will be out of line
ok
(person sitting- here's a quarter)
thank you
sit down until we call you.
(Go to locker and cannot figure it
out..person helps and asks if this is
your first time?)
yes
(it gets better)

Byfield
Yes
Take off shoes
(Points)
put them in the basket.
(no answer-just looks)
(puts shoes in basket,
go through security).
spread eagle
excuse me
spread eagle
are you a felon?

no
do you have contraband?
no
any drugs, or paraperhenlia
no(thought isn't that contraband)
ever worked
for the correctional facility
no
go sit
do you know how long the wait
nope, just wait, where are you going,
ha ha
30 minutes later,
you can go
go where
down the hall
(security at the end of the hall)
hand
excuse me
PUT HAND ON TABLE
there is no mark
excuse me
a mark
a mark
they did not put a mark on your hand
wait over there until they come.
security comes sorry give me your
hand
(stamps hand)

hand
(puts hand on table)
ok, go stand at door
door opens
moves to the next door
door opens
guard, seeing who
Michael
go sit anywhere
sit down,
can't sit there
where do you want me to sit
over there
can't sit close to inmate must be
across
30 minutes later
Son comes out
Hi mom
Hi son
How are you?
Fine
No problem getting through
No
Everything is all right
how are you doing?

PRISON VISIT 3

Number
&@#)*
here's my id
not yet
sorry
sign in
yes
id
here
call you
thanks
ready
no stamp

excuse me
you did not stamp me
sorry
you do not have to
spread eagle
Are you a felon?
Nope
do you have contraband?
no
any drugs, or paraphenia
no(thought isn't that contraband)
ever worked for the correctional fa-
cility
no
feet
excuse me
feet
what about my feet
show us your feet
(hold feet up)
no soles
you want to see the soles of my feet
yep
show soles
why
EXCUSE ME
just curious why
rules
alright
through
(I go sit down)
why are you sitting?
waiting for you to call
this is early morning
you do not have to wait
thanks
(go down the hall)
hand
thanks
door
thanks
door

thanks
here for Michael
sit at table ten
thanks
30 minutes later
hi mom,
hi Michael
how are you
fine mom, how are you
fine, all is well

OLD SCHOOL/NEW SCHOOL

was at church
when old school
was talking to
young blood
about the place
in Chi-Town
where the jazz was good,
weed was free,
rap was socio-politically relevant, &
sex was open.
I turn and said
the Point!
He said yes,
shocked that the
preacher knew.
I smiled
cause I remembered
the REV-VO-LUT-SHUN.

WHO IS CHE?

I knew my Black behind
was old when
Peter gave me
A Che Guevara journal
he got in Paris,
and young hip hoppers
so called church revolutionaries
talking about radicalism
asked me who was Che?

I AM WOMAN

SACRIFICING OURSELVES

In discussion with a pastor about a lectionary text, he commented that members in his bible class challenged his interpretation about a particular scripture and he was reluctant to preach it. His concern was that he would see their faces and hear their voices knowing they disagreed with his position and he found it difficult to preach. While his interpretation of the scripture was clearly correct, I was drawn more by the lack of assurance of his preaching and knowledge, and questioned it. The foundational concern was do you always preach wondering what the people will think or feel about your interpretation? I gave my thoughts on leadership, confidence, not seeing their faces, the usual rah rah, etc...

Later, I realized how prone we are to sacrifice tangibles as evidence of our discipline. During various seasons such as Lent, we follow strict diets, take candy, caffeine, and cursing out of our lives and yet some of the deeper areas are neglected. I laughed when God reminded me of how I was like this preacher. I have allowed what people thought, said, or how I perceived their looks to be distractions to the power within and the fulfillment of God's purpose in my life.

While I may have worked through most of these issues in my preaching, there were so many other ways that I slowed up, stepped back or delayed what God had given me. Many of us live with some of these anxieties as leaders in denominational or corporate settings, because we feel who we are appears to be very different than the status quo and we wonder how we fit in with our gifts.

We see the faces, hear the voices, and wonder if we match what we think the greater community desires. As women, the lack of mentors often hinders us as well, and we try to follow a script that God did not write for us. We begin imitating others male or female or worse crafting some aloof, uncooperative, judgmental stance to hide our fears.

The truth is while we do live in greater community, our greatest asset is the authenticity of being who we are and are called to be. This alone will encourage interpersonal relationships and serves as fortitude for our endurance.

Some thing will have to die before we live the fullness of our authenticity. What will you need to sacrifice? Could it be procrastination in prayer and indiscipline to get the daily-ness of your life and projects ordered? Is it exercise to keep body, mind and spirit energized and healthy, or mental exercises to remind you that you are fearfully and wonderfully made. For some, it is the releasing of bad memories, words and actions that hurt and hinder. It is living your best life and calling yourself woman everyday with the assurance that you are bold, brilliant and beautiful.

Calling yourself woman represents that you are developed in the arsenal of faith, fired in the belly of survival, made in the image of the ordinary that lived extraordinary lives. Marian Anderson states that "fear is a disease that eats away at logic and makes man (woman) inhuman". You are not inhuman and certainly not fearful when you walk with God.

Decide now how far you will be at the end of a season of a personal quest to live out your visions and dreams. How much will your sacrifices of personal repentance from the culture of failure allow you to move to the next level beyond facebook hype, rhetoric with your friends or pseudo ritualism of positive thinking?

During this season what a great opportunity to refocus your energy to live beyond the limitations and frustrations of corporate and denominational settings where you can lose all sense of personal accountability, responsibility and personality to meet every changing standard. Yes, you work and live in these environments but God gives grace so that we do not continue to compromise who God and you are.

Let's find that grace and sacrifice our pride, anger, ego, fears, anxieties, frustrations, internal dis-ease and unrest to draw closer to God. Let's trust the voice of God and live out the truth that we are created in the image of God and are strong, bold and brilliant. This time we can do this. It begins today, right now, with sacrifice and commitment. Finish the dream. Live, Learn, and Lead...unleash your talent! You will do this.

WOMEN NURTURERS...WOMEN WARRIORS

Did anyone get the press release that women were only relegated to one station in life? Did you?

That we had to choose between mother, lover, adventurer, employee, or warrior?

Who decided that in God's original design women were created to be subservient to men and only have babies?

Certainly God did not.

We are created in the image of God. Powerful, able to subdue the enemy, dominate the world, multiply, and think.

Did you get this so called announcement that it is inappropriate and incapable for women to think outside the box?

We can't think without someone's guidance.
Who said so?

I was raised by and around real women who were nurturers and warriors.

Women who when they walked in the room, had presence.
Not because they were cute and dainty but self assured.
In their day would make Janet Jackson stop dancing, Ciara put some clothes on and Lil Kim cry.

Real women who traveled around the world.
Had the finest jewelry.
Took you to the best restaurants.
Knew philosophy and practiced astrology.
When you were around them, you could imagine Japan, Turkey, Kenya and Egypt...

Did you remember Grandma who could take one chicken and feed the whole family and make a sweet potato pie blindfolded?
They always smelled like cinnamon, rosemary, and Mogen David wine still managing to be the first woman supervisor at the plant.
She was bold, sassy, and funny and did not allow you to read the press release.

Through her legacy you have become a woman nurturer and warrior.

Now you are intimidated
only by the potential of your greatness.
Wondering if the light on the ocean
is the reflection of the stars
or the brightness of your own soul.
Finally, feeling that it is not arrogant
to look in the mirror and say Hmmm, not bad,...
pretty good.
Enjoying the loudness of the silence around you because you can make your
music without accompaniment.
Make the best macaroni and cheese
while reading the Wall Street Journal, Black Enterprise and Jet magazine.
Knowing which weave hair is the best to buy.
Can look good in jeans and Jill S.
Ain't scared of your own children.
Certainly no longer afraid of life
although you know what it means
to struggle and juggle and
wear a momma hat,
wife/girlfriend hat,
boss hat,
secretary hat,
and holy woman hat.
Singing Precious Lord
better than Aretha
and when church is over,
have your child or significant other ask
...uh..what's for dinner?
You cook, clean, wash, love, hate, forgive, angst,
own your own business, finish school, volunteer, stumble in life, a change
agent.
Now, a woman nurturer and woman warrior.

Judges 4: Deborah and Yael

IS THERE A SISTER IN THE HOUSE?

Is there a sister in the house?
A caring and sharing;
Living and giving;
Believing and bearing;
Sister in the house?

a sister from the Nile?
a sister from the Isles;
a black and tall,
brown and short,
cream and sweet,
sister in the house?

Is there a sister in the house?
A curly hair, long hair,
short hair, natural hair
fried and slapped to the side,
can't-do-nothing with her hair sister.
an older sister in the house?

A Momma/ Grandmomma/ Big Momma
raising one child, five children, ten children;
None going to jail children.
Humiliated by Miss Ann so you can go home and hug Little Anne.
Taking in clothes, sewing clothes, washing clothes;
Fixing hand-me-down clothes,
so that our children would not have rag clothes.
Using the feet of pigs, the ground of beef,
the backs of chickens
to give our children some food.
Loving a man who loved you
but could not hold you
sister in the house?

Trusting when tried...
Praying when unprotected;
Believing when beaten;
Going on when your son was shot,
daughter raped,
and your family does not understand

why you keep humming
the Lord will make a way somehow.

Are you a sister in the house?
who's praying for the unsaved;
Healing the sick;
Fighting against racism/ sexism.
Is there a sister in house?

A hurting sister in the house?
            mocked by white women,
raped by white men;
            misunderstood by Black men;
Backstabbed by your sisters,
only trusting Jesus and yourself.

Sisters who do not know the strength of your mothers who have stopped trust-
ing Christ and started believing in crack?

Sisters with HIV/AIDS/battered/bruised in a relationship that you love but can-
not stand.
Losing our own children to murder,
gangs, sex, violence, drugs, and an I am my own boss philosophy.
Losing our sacred seed to the gospel according to the Hip Hop Culture.
Imitating the lunacy of Ludacris,
nonsense of 50 cents,
following into the 1-2 step of Ciara
and dressing like Lil Kim.

Are you scared of your own children
afraid of your shadow
nervous about your future
distrusting the church and community?
Is there a sister in the house?

Is there a sister who wants to be healed,
get strength out of weakness,
work for your spiritual and physical liberation?
Let's get busy.
Let's get strong.

Rizpah

SUPER WOMAN

Do you ever wonder who these
super women really are
who have time to cook marvelous meals,
keep a super clean house,
decorate with flowers they made themselves,
having time to go out and take the world?
I know they exist
but how many sisters you know
even after getting the children
ready for school the night before
wake up hearing junior say
I forget we got a field trip today
we have to bring our lunch
and I need ten dollars for the entrance.
Little Amy is crying
I don't want to wear the purple blouse
I want the pink one, the same pink one
she wore yesterday.
You have to prepare
for a breakfast meeting
with your supervisor and
trying to figure out
how to find ten dollars you do not have
And lunch meat with your health conscious self
How do super women handle it
when the boss says you have to stay late today
when the after school closes at 6 pm
and you can't get the baby daddy or your parents on the phone?
Do you ever wonder who these super women really are?
Who look good,
act well,
own their businesses ,
have perfectly wonderfully balanced children
with a loving husband to boot.
All you just want is to go to the movies
without it being a Broadway production to get there.
Not a vacation to an isle
But a trip to the bathroom
with a calgon moment
without someone saying,

honey, momma or the phone is ringing.
You are just a woman on the job
who realizes that
buying silk flower arrangements ain't a sin.
purchasing rotisserie chicken ain't a crime,
and having dirty dishes in the sink
won't send you to hell.
It's ok to be imperfect
and not always be a super woman.

TAKE A BOW

If a nobel prize
was given
to a woman who:
Speaks her mind...effectively,
knows what she believes...mightily,
has a sense of humor....wickedly,
is a friend...earnestly,
cooks and entertains...splendidly,
lives life joyously, and abundantly,
overcomes problems.. prayerfully,
stands beside her mate.... passionately, and wisely,
loves her children.. unconditionally,
gives of herself... liberally,
maintains her home with gracious hospitality,
breathes in harmony
with community,
and serves God faithfully,
you would be the first in line.

Take a bow!

Yvonne and Mita

HOW DOES A WOMAN RESPOND TO EVIL

How does a woman
respond to the
conditions of this world?
a holy woman
dressed to kill
with the right ascent
(scarf and pin)

How does a woman respond
after you have gotten your hair done
and nails airbrushed
and your Mary Kay facial?

What do you do with sin,
crime,
poverty,
neglect,
political injustice,
racism,
sexism,,
and HIV/AIDS?
after
your meetings,
night of prayer,
day of fasting,
the Annual convention/Spring workshop?

What do you do with evil?
I mean sho nuff,
down home,
makes you want
to throw up your hands
and holler evil.

Conditions that are sickening,
make you mad,
get you down, and
make you want to give up.
make you scared,
intimidate you, and

tear you apart
that you become as evil as
evil.

How does a woman respond to the destruction of our children,
HIV/AIDS,
insidious,
diabolical,
evil?

THE RAPING

You called it a sport
For three minutes
Overpowering me
Demanding what I detested
Causing physical and emotional pain
While you enjoyed 3 minutes of
brute
bestial
Pleasure
effecting a life time of rape
Over and over because
You raped my mind
trust
security
and inner strength
long after
your three minutes.

Today
I choose to take
back my strength
and
win the game.

A MOTHER'S MOAN

The moan of a mother
in the loss of a child
is more painful than
any sob
or cry.

It represents the loss
of life,
vision,
creation,
a part of self.

WOMAN

I call myself woman
because I was taken
from someone's rib
to live on my own inner power.
fired in the belly of survival,
developed in the arsenal of strength,
feasted on the fountain of faith,
I have learned that
If I am strong enough
enhance life/to bring forth life/support life
I am strong enough to live.

I AM
COMMUNITY

TRYING TO MAKE LOGIC OUT OF ILLOGIC

Every time we see a murder on a school campus or senseless murders at a work place, we are devastated by the news and impact. There is a lifetime of grief and pain for families, friends, the institution and the nation. We are united in a heinous crime.

Death at any level is overwhelming. Random senseless murders are beyond words. We consider our high school and college campuses reasonably safe, certainly not places of murder.

Murder has become a logical option for the illogical. Hatred and violence have taken over the lives of so many and we seem impotent to stop violence of any kind.

Blaming has been prevalent the last few years and the media has overwhelmed us with theory and reason other than meanderings of an unchecked mentally ill person. The gun laws are too lenient for their supporters, and for others, they are not the cause. It must be the violence on television, in movies or video games or an institution or people who knew these persons were ill. There must be a logical reason.

You cannot make logic out of illogic. In the midst of death, there is life. Life matters whether it is with thousands touched by the on campus deaths or gang related murders that, annually, quadruple school deaths. We cannot forget the blood bath of those in the Middle East for whom this country bears some responsibility, the millions dying from AIDS or the thousands living in neglect, poverty, and abuse.

Where do we go from here? We work to activate continued peace, healing and forgiveness in the heartaches of all families whose lives have been unalterably changed. We work to positively affect lives so they know that someone cares and is listening while working on the conditions that allow these types of crimes. Somewhere there is someone who is already plotting to top this and we must touch them with the love of God.

If nothing else, these murders have shown us to enjoy life and your family daily. Realize that even in pain God is present. Pray without ceasing. Forgive immediately. Read your Bible regularly. Laugh, love and live. The next day is not promised.

THIS IS OUR PROMISE

(at the funeral of Lisa and her four children bludgeoned by her boyfriend and father of one of the children)

This is our promise.
Lisa and your little ones
hear us
and hear us well.
Forget any suggestion
that this is a one day event.
Erase any theory
that we will not remember.
Ignore any speculation
that we will not fight.
We can not
bring you back
Lisa and your little ones.
We can not promise
that another one,
will not be
abused,
beaten,
or killed.
We declare that one by one
we will breathe in life,
war in the spirit,
grab a child,
hold a woman,
confront a violator
until the silence of your screams
erupt in thunderous roars,
saying
no more,
no more,
no more.

Let there be no surprise,
no hesitation,
no faltering,
no miscalculation.
the church will not

be silent any more
will not passively
let the screams
be snuffed or
dismiss families in torment.
Lisa and your little ones
hear and hear us well.
This is our promise
empowered by the God
we serve,
love,
who loves us,
sent Jesus to die for us,
and rose again for us.
will carry us
through to
break all barriers,
restore order
integrity,
still violence,
heal families
until justice
rolls down as waters
and righteousness
as a mighty stream;
and Jesus returns to reign forever-
more.
This is our promise.
No more.
No more.
No more.

HAVE YOU EVER BEEN WRONGED?

Have you ever been wronged?
When no one understands
why you are angry.
keeps telling you to let it go.
Get over it.
It's not that deep.
But you can't
because you were just wronged
and it is that deep.

You just want your voice heard,
a place to complain
and no one seems to hear,
understand
you have been wronged.

One day you will get over it
but right, now, you have lost your job
when you were innocent,
got a reprimand when you did not violate the rule.
The lawyer stole your money.
The teacher lied on you.
The neighbor's dog dug up your flowers again.
You just want some fairness….
some justice.

The system will not treat you right.
The judge will not even listen to you.
The court keeps postponing your case
The appellate court turned you down.
The attorney refuses to return your call.
The police do not believe you have been violated.
Your momma does not believe that the teacher lied on you.
You can't get over it/past it
because you have been wronged
and no one understands why you are angry;
Well you are downright mad
and even if you lose the case, that would be ok,
at least you had a fair hearing.
You just want justice.

Luke 18.

DISARMED
For a friend who is HIV infected

You disarm me with your smile.
Just your smile
when I know behind the smile
the pain overwhelms.

You are not just sick,
you are sick with HIV
and can't tell anyone.
The abandonment is too great,
disapproval is too strong
the church where you
had the relationship
with the brother preacher
would turn its back on you.

Yet you disarm me with your smile.
Just because of your smile
when I know behind the smile
there is hope even in the midst of pain.

Please rest while I bless you.
There are some of us who care,
love unconditionally
and know that in God's infinite mercy
this is not God's cause.
But as an agent of God
let me disarm you with my love
which is God's love
and walk together with you
and find a place where we can both smile.

JUST A THOUGHT

Do you think God wants us to stay
in relationships with men
who forget to whom
they are married
and think casual sex
is recreational?
always responding
" I don't know
it just happened."

Because they only did it once
is not a justification
for continual forgiveness
only to find out that their once
is once a week with a different person.
Molebesha this week,
Karenan last week
and Bill on the down low
but he luvs …….you.

Is it possible that life
while painful in its transition
is better than this crap?
Being alone is more accommodating
than sleeping single in a double bed
with a man who never comes in anyway.
bringing you his stuff,
his diseased stuff,
no attention stuff,
lying/ cheating stuff,
no paycheck stuff,
often no sex stuff.
You know the brother is
tired from all that 'work" .

You can have your own stuff
of peace, calm , joy, and strength
moving toward your unity and
pursuing your own greatness
and wholeness.

Just a thought my sister.
Do you think God wants you to stay?
What cha think?

DECISION

You hit me once,
I blamed me.
You hit me twice,
I cried.
You hit me again,
you die.

SILENCE

Has the church figured out
that its silence on sexual abuse
is one of the reasons
why we are getting sued,
having members leave,
children affected
with silent tears
wondering
when the church will speak
with action not words.

CONTROL

You speak all over the country.
He does not let you finish
a sentence.

You drive hundreds of miles,
but he tells you how to park.

You manage hundred
of thousands of dollars.
He tells you how to count.

You manage hundreds of people.
He shows you how to wash dishes.

You call it love.
I call it stupid control.

Return the Gift!

The gift that God gives is life.
The gift that we give is to
live,
love,
laugh,
learn,
and
leave
a good legacy.

I LOVE AND AM LOVED

LIFE MATTERS

Little children, you are from God, and have conquered them; for the one who is in you is greater than the one who is in the world. Beloved, let us love one another, because love is from God... John 4: 4 and 7.

Each year we commemorate the anniversary of the Hurricane Katrina Event. Each year I think I will be able to write this without the same exhaustive emotion I had the year before. I am wrong. So many lives have been given, homes lost, a city impacted and families still apart. Death from a hurricane is one thing. Death by human disregard is another particularly when it is from governmental leaders.

Like many of you this is profoundly personal. We know this region. It was a favorite place to visit. We have relatives and friends who are affected. My brother, Bishop C. Garnett Henning lost every thing but the clothes on his back. Several AME Churches and members were lost in the Gulfport Mississippi/New Orleans area.

Yet there is hope. Death is never God's last word. Some form of rebirth is here. God created the universe out of chaos. Life emerges from death. Jesus rose from the grave. There is no natural disaster that stops God from redeeming his people and times.

God also confronts us to respond. We must resolve never to forget what happened. We must remember those who died needlessly and those who gave their lives so that others were saved. Remember those who are still emotionally, physically, spiritually and financially impacted.

We also must work for peace and restoration. There must be a resolve to be our brothers/sisters keepers here in Indianapolis and beyond. We must share our resources with those who need them and are trustworthy. You are a philanthropist when you share what you have with others.

There are children, elderly, and homeless who require our unconditional love. There are others who are grieving who need comforting. Politicians need to be challenged who are not responsive and responsible, while we register people to vote. Right here, right now there are families who are impacted by the murders and violence in Indianapolis. Get the picture. There is no time to waste. Life matters.

It is more than trite to say just pray, but pray we must. We must intercede for continued peace. Pray for God's will to be manifested and

God's strength for children whose lives have been unalterably changed. Pray that we no longer participate in activities in which we destroy people with our actions. Allow God to have full control of your thoughts and actions. Forgive immediately. Life is too short. Finally, pray that the spirit of divisiveness, arrogance, competition and jealousy is destroyed in the body of Christ.

Charity begins at home. Enjoy life and your family as much as you can. Hug them often. Tell them daily how much you love and appreciate them. Be sensitive to God's creation. Be your brothers/sisters' keepers. Give, bless, laugh, love and live. Life matters.

FOR A BLACK FATHER

For a Black father
who wants to
raise a Black man
….in America
to
love his momma,
appreciate sisters,
respect elders,
trust his father,
walk with integrity,
be
strong and sensitive,
whole and well
with a
worshipful and warrior spirit
embracing his Blackness
making a difference
in his environment
loving God and becoming
a good father himself.

SHOUT OUT TO BLACK FATHERS

This poem is not for everyone
It is for a Black father.
Real fathers.
Not hollywood movie
or television sitcom dads.

You are a loving father
who knows what it means to give him up
to a world who will
look at him as he walks by
in an Armani Suit and Bali tie
and still grab their pocketbooks
or hold their pants pockets.

Trying to explain to his momma
that you want him
strong and sensitive,
charming and caring,
tough and tender,
capable and able,
but a man
not a baby
when he is 12.

You cry at night at his bed
because you love him so and
are so thankful that God gave him to you.
But if the truth is told
you are scared to death that
he will not grow up whole and strong.
Surrendered to the Lord
hearing God's voice
and trusting in himself
and God to be
man.

WHAT MAKES MOTHERS SO STRONG

What makes mothers so strong?
Mothers who endured for all generations
exist for all ages.
Wiser than historical sages.
What makes mothers so strong?

Raising families,
loving children,
washing, cooking, cleaning.
Still giving life meaning.
Living and giving
in God believing.
What really makes a mother so strong?

Is it her foundation of work?
her legacy of family love?
faith in God above?
An inner strength
that we cannot define,
the smack of your behind?
An impacting love
that we loudly proclaim?
The power of her grace
and disarming charm?
What makes mothers so strong?

MOMMA SAID

"Ok, let's get this straight. I am the mother, you the child.,
Eat everything on your plate because there are starving children in China.
Boy/girl, I will knock you in the middle of next week.
I don't need a dishwasher, I got one.
A hard head makes for a soft behind.
Before I let the police kill you, I will kill you myself.
Girl/boy put on some Vaseline , your legs are ashy.
I'll give you your opinion when I am ready for it.
Was I talking to you? This is a grown-up folks conversation.
Take that ragged underwear off you never know when a car may hit you.
Boys/girls are like buses if you miss this one,
wait a few minutes, and another one will be by soon.
Let's get the order right.
You finish high school, go to college,
get married,
get a job,
put some money in the bank,
then you can think about getting married,
having sex,
and then a baby.

I don't care if everyone else is doing it, you ain't doing it.
I brought you in the world, I will take you out."

SOME FATHERS STAY

There are some men
who never left their children
even when they left their mommas.
Working two jobs
to handle the child's support.
Taking the abuse
from the momma's family
so they could see their children
cause they never knew their father
and remembering the mistakes
they wish they could forget.

MY MAN

*My man
is a balanced brother
a chicken and caviar eating,
Marsalis, Rachmaninoff and Kirk Franklin listening,
Walter Mosley, and Cornel West reading,
Spike Lee and Spielberg watching,
smart as Henry Louis Gates,
plays like Tiger Woods, Lebron James and A ROD together,
rugged as Morgan Freeman,
fine as Morris Chestnut,
righteous like Michael Eric Dyson,
kisses me like no other.*

ECSTASY

*My being comes alive
with your caress.
My body smiles at your
touch then groans
at the release.
I wonder if you really know
what you do to me?
But if I knew
you loved me,
I could reach ecstasy.*

MUTUALITY

You're right
I love you.
I know you love me too,
but you still got to
get the hell up out of here
with your love and all.
Yeah... you do.

FRIEND

I would like to be the friend
that you have been to me.
A presence in absence
listening when I'm not speaking,
hearing what I don't say
reachable in distance, and
in spirit.
Considerate when overlooked,
a friend beyond limitations ,
and with whom my
transparency is affirmed.
Always praying,
loving,
giving
making my life more
meaningful and full.

DAY BREAK

Day break-
I'm awake.
The sun is shining-
but not for me.
You are gone-
but sadly
will return.

MOMMA MY GRANDMOMMA

Momma....my grandmomma
could take one chicken and
feed the whole family
make a sweet potato pie blindfolded
always smelling like cinnamon,
rosemary and
Mogen David wine
worked as a maid
while becoming a
neighborhood political activist
becoming successful
at whatever she chose to do
raising six strong children
several grandchildren.
bold,
sassy,
funny,
loving ,
told you that you could
be/do/be/come whatever
you wanted
just work
pray
treat people
with respect.

I AM SPIRIT

ARE WE MISGUIDED?

One of my favorite examples of a corporate creative mistake is the McDonald's commercial for the debut of the McChicken. Several years ago, there was an advertising hype for the emergence of the fried McDonald's wings. The commercial featured an African American marching band with majorettes singing and dancing in the old "buck dance" tradition "we luv McChicken...oooo McChicken".

There was a strong outrage regarding the use of African Americans to foster stereotypes. The very object of selling a good product was lost because the commercial insulted the audience it targeted. Moreover, such thoughtlessness was uncommon from McDonalds.

Where were the quality control persons? Did not the dancers understand the impact? Everyone thought it was a good idea, but it had repercussions that caused McDonalds to scrap months of planning of a good product and an economic windfall. There certainly was a better way to sell the product.

Do we exhibit similar behaviors in the religious community? We are trying to reach our target community and misunderstand what actually appeals. Do we insult them without really measuring the impact of stereotypes, clichés and inappropriate communication? Obviously no one told McDonald's that black youth buck dancing would offend people or they foolishly thought that it would not matter. What seemed to be a good idea was an insult to the people they were trying to please.

In our zest to build new buildings or initiate new projects, we often develop financial schemes; diminish the house with chitterlings and catfish as the sole way in which the funds are raised. Instead of the sacrificial giving and the obedience to tithe, we reduce the word of God.

Several years ago, while on an elevator I said, "Good morning" to a brother wearing his church's tee shirt. He bellowed, "Praise the Lord, my sister! Praise the Lord! Not good morning, Praise the Lord!" "How are you?" he said. I responded, "Fine, thank you." He said, "No! Blessed, my sister. Blessed! You are blessed by the best. Say it. Blessed!" The elevator stopped at my floor and I did not respond. What a misguided witness! This wonderful brother believed he was really being a good witness by correcting me on my greeting. I was amused, others would not have been.

We often do the same with those in need of our witness. Our tone can be insulting missing the mark of genuine love and care. Learn from McDonalds, and know that if it is the customer (unsaved) we are trying to please (reach), let us be responsible in our language and witness.

WHY DO SOME SURVIVE?

Why do some people survive
and others do not?
What is it that causes
some to go on,
pray ,
live
when others throw in the towel,
and tear down the racks?
Why do some people survive?
Make it through great obstacles,
run through the firing line,
escape from the lion's den,
stand the test of the fire.
Others at the smell of the fire,
thought of the lions,
hear about a firing line
go back on drugs,
kill their mommas
their fool selves
because they cannot see a way out.

Why do some not survive
eat their young,
give up hope,
jump off cliffs,
or walk through life
as if they are zombies.
Get depressed,
withdraw because
something did not go right,
someone betrayed them
or life was not ordered in their favor.

Why did some jump off the ship,
die at the smell of the death of fellow slaves?
While others ran away,
spat in their master's food
or killed them.
Some lived through it,
praying and hoping

for the day of freedom.
What is the culturalization,
socialization,
spirituality,
that someone says come hell
or high water,
nothing will stop me.
If I fall I will just get back up.
Knocked down not knocked out.
Fall back is just a step back
for a come back.

What makes
some people say
I trust in God
I trust in me
and this too shall pass.
Until then I will keep on fighting
until times get better.
Why do some survive?

HOW BIG

Is your God big enough to do
more than an occasional answering of a prayer?
Meeting basic needs and cares;
Making you feel good
when you have a tear or a sigh;
is your God big enough
to truly give you the desires of your heart?
Confronting the demons of your life;
Effecting change beyond yourself;
And doing more than you ask or think?
How big is your God?

ASSERTIVELY AND AGGRESSIVELY MEDIOCRE

What happened?
Can someone tell me when
laziness, triflinness,
and slothfulness
became the norm?
Surely someone knows the date
when it became ok for
too-low pants,
too-high skirts, halters,
and thongs to be seen in public.
When girls wearing words on their behinds,
teenage girls with purple hair;
and men wearing hats
in church became acceptable.
Now grand mommas are wearing hot pants and
big poppas are wearing big crosses on low opened shirts with gray hair.
Help me somebody!
When did the church
sanction bad behavior,
low living,
no reading,
no trying,
no manners,
and no respect
for elders,
people,
and God.
Come on now
it must have passed me by.
I woke up one day
and Good God
there it was.
Black people
were just like everyone else.
Everybody was named
Isha: Modesha, Glodesha, and Bonesha
Or Quar: you know
Jenaiquar, Goodequar, and Boodalouguar
names we can not spell or pronounce.
Or worse naming our children after cars:

Lexus, Mercedes, and Porsche.
The last time I checked we were told
that nakedness was not acceptable,
disrespecting our parents was cause for death,
average was unthought of,
people like George W. Bush 1 & 2,
a two bit actor like Ronald Reagan
would never have become president;
and a misguided prophet,
using racism as a platform for bad religion,
like Pat Roberson would never have been
sanctioned by black folks.
Now we got young preachers
who have not lived much longer
than the creation of the computer
parroting such nonsense
agreeing that Haiti had an earthquake
because of voodooism.
If that is the case, why hasn't
America been destroyed? We sin.
Hmmmm, I tell you. I missed it.
The revelation, the proclamation, the unveiling ceremony
when the church become like everyone else,
and we patterned our visions on the average.
Everyone got to have the same ministries
even when there is no anointing or talent;
sitting on the front row or the pulpit and
being an officer or preacher makes us so "important"
that serving ain't even on our mind.
When did every preacher have to look like a bishop
with their own entourage?
Licentiates have preaching portfolios, business cards
and ministries separate from the church;
television evangelists who misrepresent the word
manipulating the people becomes the norm.
And the church and the community do not feel it necessary
to support, help, love those with purple hair,
too low pants and too high skirts.
Forgetting that the church was the one place
where professor and prostitute could sit on the pew
declaring we are sinners saved by grace.
The churches set the standard not follow the world

and it was the place where you learned
to love your neighbor as you love yourself.
Can someone help me?
When did we become aggressively and
assertively mediocre?

GOD'S HUMOR

There are times in which I think
God has a warped sense of humor
more creative than movies
more imaginative than science fiction.
There are some things in life
that are just funny.
Not ha, ha, but peculiar.
All you can do is look up at God and say,
what's up with this?
God created the duckbill platypus and called it good,
500 types of grass of which we are allergic,
gave us resources which we will not use,
strength and we walk in fear,
prosperity in scarcity,
healing in sickness,
intelligence when we choose ignorance,
power when the world is fainting,
gifts that go unused and unappreciated.
God created humanity,
male and female in God's image,
gave us control and dominion over the world
yet before the foundation of the world,
told Jesus to be prepared to go and save us
for we are going to walk in disobedience
kill our goofy selves and
end up in the dungeon of our lives
but then he said he would forgive us
and restore us even in the dungeon
if we would just ask.
God has a strange sense of humor.

IN THE WORDS OF SCOOBY DOO... HUUH?

Have you heard preachers
who preach justice,
teach that all of God's people are
created equal,
and will not let women in the pulpit
or allow any difference
or tolerate any thing
that is not limited to their beliefs?
In the words of Scooby Doo... HuuH

Preachers who preach
that it is time for these young girls
to stop being sexually active
but will flirt with a sixteen-year-old.

How about church people who get all teary eyed
at I love the Lord he heard my cry
and pitied every groan
long as I live and troubles rise,
I'll hasten to his throne.
But will not pray,
come to prayer meeting,
and get mad if the preacher prays too long
Huuh?

How about church people who believe
that the problems of the world
would be fixed if the church
would just bring back that old time religion.
See if we would sing that good music,
you know let Mount Zion rejoice,
or read the Ten Commandments every Sunday;
Make every body follow good old Biblical principles
the church will be just fine.
Cause then we did not have any problems.

But those same people cannot find the Ten Commandments
in the Bible.
Do not know if it is the Old or New Testament.
Cannot distinguish between Chronicles and Corinthians

and when they see the Book Hosea
think it is the Spanish book in the Bible.

They have forgotten when they were bored
in the same church they call good.
And at the age of 70
are having unprotected and unordained sex
with other so called good old down home Christians.

Church people who say this is us's church.
We need more people.
We need more programs.
We need more money.
But will run anybody away who's new or
looks different or worse just ignore them.
Will not allow anything new in the church
and will not come out to an afternoon program on a bet.
Will continue to give one dollar as their giving.
Come to church mad just because
and leave mad just because.

Same church people who love their church,
love God
but will not tithe or
will march down to the tithing box and
put two dollars in it.
Will hurt somebody if
they think the preacher has spent the dollar they gave.

Will allow their good church to die
because they will not fix up,
remodel,
rebuild, or
restore.

Sing More Love to Thee O Christ
and can not work with bro so and so,
speak to sis so and so,
forgive some one for a simple error,
fight someone who moves a pew,
or change something that their great granny started
35 years ago.

Sing Our God is an awesome God but
don't believe in divine healing
or divine retribution.
In the words of Scooby Doo... huuh?

YOU WANNA BE HEALED

Are you tired of not living beyond your limitation;
staying at the proverbial door of failure;
masking a smile with internal pain and shame;
moving but making no progress;
advancing to the back of the line
while carrying the same pain,
the same wounds,
the same hurts,
and making the same mistakes
that you end up at the
same place with the same issues.
Loving the wrong person
over and over because
you are the one sick.
Wanting more money and then
overspending on stupid stuff then
wanting some more money again.
Mistarts yet again.
Now you are not sure
that you can answer
you wanna be healed.

WHAT MAKES GOD SO MAD?

Have you ever wondered what makes God so angry?
Ticks God the Father off?
I mean gets so mad that God loses God's cool,
erupts a blood vessel,
sends his pulse racing.
Makes God curse.
Has God throw up both God's hands and holler.
What makes God mad?
What causes God's wrath?
God's headache?
God's impatience that God says, "Enough.
I am filing for a divorce,
ending the deal,
destroying your behavior,
wishing that I had never made you".
What is it that gets God's dander up
and causes God to kill people?
We sing about the goodness of God
and his mercy endures forever.
God is a forgiving God,
healing God, loving God.
What about the angry God?
The Mad God?
The unhappy God?
What do we do when God gets mad?

Have you thought about what you have done to make God mad?
What sin, what behaviors,
actions, words, and thoughts?
What lies in you to send his blood pressure boiling?
Today is the day.
The first day of all days
for the rest of your life to decide
I will not make God mad.
Rub him the wrong way,
tick him off, and burn his flipper.
Today, I confess my ingratitude,
my selfishness,
my sinfulness.
I want to get right with God.

REMEMBER WHEN CHURCH WAS JUST CHURCH!

There wasn't the praise church,
the Holy Ghost church,
or the teaching church.
It was just church.

You were either Baptist,
Methodist, or Holy Roller.
And on any given day,
you just went to church.

Remember when there was
no BUPPY Church,
or Blue-Collar church;
Except for maybe the Congregational
and the Episcopalian church...remember?

Remember when we did not have
any classes on praise and worship,
prayer;
Classes on being a missionary
or serving?

If it was time to pray,
you just prayed.
Some prayed silently.
Some prayed aloud.
Others just said, "Oh Lord."
Remember?

Remember when we did not have
to be an expert on the Bible
to be a Christian?
We did not have
to know every Hebrew
and Greek meaning.
Lay people did not have
concordances, commentaries,
or Bible dictionaries.
We just read the Bible.
Remember?

Remember when doctors and lawyers
went to the same church
as domestic workers?
The only concern was if
you were Methodist or Baptist...

While everyone was proud
of the doctor
and proud of the teacher;
On Sunday morning,
everyone was brother or sister;
Or just Tom and Anne.
Church was the one place
where Miss Anne and Annie Mae
could work together,
pray together, and
sing together.
Remember?

Poor and rich,
PhD and GED, sitting on the same trustee boards.
Former drug addicts and doctors, sitting on the same pew.
Church ladies who commented on everyone.
Ushers who could stop a locomotive with their gloves.
Never smiling when they gave you a worship guide.
Remember?

Young people screaming 'Oh Happy Day' off key.
Older people singing 'Let the Daughters of Judah be Glad'.
* Preachers even without a sermon caused the people to lose their mind*
with a good hoop and a tune.
Remember?

It was just one church
and when there was a crisis
everyone responded.
There was focus,
concern, and love.

Remember?
Let's work to have church again.

WHERE ARE YOU GOD?

Where are you God
when evil is aggravating,
people are agitating,
daughters are in Iraq,
government is corrupt,
I can't get a job,
my man's downlow,
drugs/diseases overflow,
violence is choking me,
the hypocrisy is bringing misery,
unfreedom,
injustice
and lack of
equality?
When we are
in pain,
sickness,
slavery
and death
where are you God?

KNOW GOD WORKS

Much like the earth
is a renewing creation,
at the scent of water,
a tree renews itself.
Seeds that are planted
have some dormancy
but soon there is life.
Know in the end,
God prevails
trust God's plan
more than anyone else.
No matter how long it takes
God works.

THIS IS MY WAKE UP CALL

Listen ungod
this is my wakeup call
I am no longer held in tyranny
by your domination
manipulated by your unwisdom
controlled by your audacity
to use me to hurt others
and me.
No longer will
my hopes be frustrated
dreams devastated
visions aggravated
faith mitigated
strength metastasized
anxieties energized
or my ability to live my best life confounded.
I have the soil of Africa in my roots
The potency of the ancestral foundation
The blood of Jesus in my veins
and the power of the Holy Spirit as my reign
I will not bow down,
back away
shrivel at your unpower,
With God I live and die.
This is my wake up call.

I AM FREE

The necessity of my sanity,
the level of my disintegration
causes a reassimilation
of me.
I no longer yearn to be in order
with you if that means
out of order with me.
Your definition of self,
identification of perfect,
standard for wholeness
holds me hostage to
your declaration of my totality.
My dissolution is over.
No more conformance to an impossible normalcy,
acceptance of other's idiosyncraticism
of my color, hips and hair.
My beauty, belief, and behavior
are all now self defined
Desiring no recognition
at my rejection.
I am finally in order with myself
and with God
which make me out of order with you
and others.

Annehenningbyfield is one who dares to **Live**, **Learn** and **Lead**.

She **live**s a life filled with creativity and passion. A psalmist, a poet and composer, she wrote the litany used for Mrs. Rosa Parks' funeral in Detroit, Michigan, and Congresswoman Julia Carson's funeral in Indianapolis. She performs in many Spoken Word settings and is currently preparing a Spoken Word CD. Her book *Issuing A New Press Release* will soon be published. She strives to live her best life daily. She is married to Ainsley and they have one son, Michael, and a grandson, Miles.

Her works include: *Let the Worship Begin, A book of Liturgy; Odyssey—A Girls Mentoring Program,* co-written with Florance M. McElroy; *Preparing Leaders for Leadership; An Adult Understanding of the Hip Hop Culture, The Church's Response to Hurricane Katrina (African American Lectionary),* and she is featured in the *4th Edition of Those Preaching Women and the Fall 2009 edition of the African American Pulpit with an article "Living Through Crisis".*

As a **learner**, she earned her Bachelor's of Science degree from Wilberforce University, attended Christian Theological Seminary, Indianapolis, and received her Masters of Divinity degree from Newburgh Theological Seminary; an Honorary Doctor of Divinity Degree from R.R. Wright School of Religion, Johannesburg, South Africa: Harvard Divinity School/School of Government Summer Leadership Program for Community Development, and Ashland Seminary's Pastors of Excellence.

As a **lead**er, she is considered both bold and brilliant. She is the president of AHB and Associates, which is a consulting firm to help clients unleash their talents. She has done extensive training and consulting in organizational transformation, leadership development, and personal executive coaching. Her clients include universities, small companies, social service agencies and others.

This includes her role as a journey coach with second time around parents, religious leaders, and other groups. Profiled in numerous newspapers, journals and books, she is included in The Trumpet to Zion (a video that explores the dynamics between the African American Church and HIV/ AIDS). She has received the King Drum Major for Peace Award and Jarena Lee Preaching Award among others.

Partnering with the Martin Luther King Center in Indianapolis, she uses her art poem and healing moments to aid the elderly finding themselves second time around parents. She is Dean of the Fourth District Board of Examiners, a member of Payne

Theological Seminary Board of Trustees, Latino/African American Dialogue Group, and Alpha Kappa Alpha Sorority and is recognized as one of the most 15 influential African Americans in the city of Indianapolis. She has preached on three continents and has preached/taught in Wesley Cathedral (John Wesley Cathedral in London, England, the Caribbean, and West and South Africa.) She is considered to be the first or one of the first women to become a presiding elder whose father was a presiding elder.

She is the presiding elder of the North District Indiana Annual Conference, and served as the presiding elder of the South District for 4 years. She has served as Senior Pastor of three churches, Bethel AME Church, Bloomington, Robinson Community AME Church, Indianapolis, and St. Paul AME Church, Detroit, MI with over 25 years of service. At every charge including the South District, spiritual, financial, numerical and community growth were realized.

annehenningbyfield

Brochures:
>Understanding Worship in AME Church
>Now That You Are Saved
>Now That You Have Joined

Books:
>Let The Worship Begin:
>Those Preaching Women Multicultural Edition:
>Issuing a New Press Release (ready spring 2010)
>Odyssey: A Girls Rite of Passage Program

Presentations/Power Points:
a. Leadership Odyssey
b. Preparing Leaders For Leadership
c. Youth Are Leaders Too
d. Ten Steps to Unleashing Your Talents
e. Understanding Worship in the AME Church:
f. An Adult Understanding of Hip Hop
g. How the Church Prepares for the Invitation
h. Living Your Best Life
i. Text or Tune
a. What is Preaching?

MANUALS
1. New Members' Manual
2. Stewards' Manual
3. Church Policy Handbook

Original Music: Anthems, Praise and Worship and Hymns. Will send catalogue on request.

Art Cards and Mouse Pads: Fusing personal poetry for life empowerment. Will send catalogue on request. Cards cover women's, men's, children and church themes.

PLEASE MAKE CHECKS PAYABLE TO

annehenningbyfield: Post Office Box 55106; Indianapolis, Indiana 46205-0106.
317 283-0140(office) 317 283-2334(fax). pehenby@aol.com;
www.annehenningbyfield.org

The
Essence
Of my
Existence

annehenningbyfield

TRUE VINE
PUBLISHING CO.